Asked for Healing

... Given Grace

Margaret James

CHRISTIAN ❖ LITERATURE ❖ CRUSADE
Fort Washington, Pennsylvania 19034

CHRISTIAN LITERATURE CRUSADE

U.S.A.
P.O. Box 1449, Fort Washington, PA 19034

GREAT BRITAIN
51 The Dean, Alresford, Hants., SO24 9BJ

AUSTRALIA
P.O. Box 91, Pennant Hills, N.S.W. 2120

NEW ZEALAND
10 MacArthur Street, Feilding

ISBN 0-87508-563-6

This printing 1998

PRINTED IN THE UNITED STATES OF AMERICA

Contents

This booklet is dedicated to

my Savior and Friend
Jesus Christ

my husband
Graham

my children
Sonja and Geoffrey Dixon
Philip and Kim James
Katie and Sean Richards
and Justin James

and all my grandchildren

Introduction

Surprising though it may be, when God gave me grace rather than healing, He intended it for good, not for evil. The accomplishment of His plan and purpose in my life is worth even more than a restoration of my health. I know the pain is not in vain. This poem written by Kenneth L. Pike expresses the same truth. It appears in the first of his five volumes of poetry: Volume 1, *On Pain: Beyond Suffering*.

Gain from Pain

Peter chose; but God overrules.
Matthew 26:34

It hurts—
I don't like it

Yes, it hurts.
You don't have
To like it.

But thank our Lord
That His will to choose
Went beyond His pain
To give us gain.

v

Preface

surprised * baffled * disappointed *
perplexed * stunned * apprehensive *
confused * puzzled * bewildered *

These were just a few of my initial reactions
to hearing the news that I have an incurable
disease.

How could I reconcile being a believer and
being continuously sick? Was I a sick Christian or just a Christian who was sick? Could
my body be sick and yet my soul be well?

What did John mean in his letter to Gaius,
*"Dear friend, I pray that you may enjoy good health
and that all may go well with you, even as your
soul is getting along well"*? (3 John v. 2)

Did John imply that Gaius' physical health was
in no way connected to his spiritual health?

Was Paul making the same distinction, in stating that outwardly he was wasting away, yet inwardly he was being renewed day by day? (2 Corinthians 4:16)

Could Peter also have been alluding to this when he affirmed that the body was merely a tent which in death would be put aside? (2 Peter 1:13)

Distinguishing the difference between body and soul helped me overcome my initial reactions. Yet this was only the tip of the iceberg; there were many other issues I needed to resolve.

Since God is all-powerful and can heal me if He wishes, how do I interpret it when He chooses not to? Does this signify He doesn't really love me? Or is it that I have sinned in some unforgivable way? Could it be due to my lack of faith?

In other words, is my sickness a sign of failure? (Initially, some people made me feel that it was!) If not, is it possible that sickness (a result of the Fall) could be part of God's plan for my life?

During the past six years I have been pondering questions like these, searching the Scriptures, and praying and meditating on the answers. Though I am far from a definitive understanding of God's attitude to long-term illness, my search has helped me come to terms with it. I pray this booklet may in some way help you.

About the Author

Margaret was born to Mary and Peder Lauridsen in Palmerston North, New Zealand, in 1938. Her four grandparents had immigrated to New Zealand from Denmark and were active members of the Lutheran community. Being the youngest of three children and a dairy farmer's daughter, Margaret learned very early to help milk the cows.

On leaving high school, Margaret trained as a school teacher, and after three years of teaching commenced a study program at the Bible College of New Zealand. It was during this time that she met her future husband, Graham James. They were married in the spring of 1964.

In 1974, Graham and Margaret became members of Wycliffe Bible Translators and that year began an assignment in Papua New Guinea — Graham as an ethnomusicologist and Margaret as coordinator of housing. At that time, their four children were 3 to 8 years old.

Ten years later, when their two eldest children had finished their schooling, Graham and Margaret were reassigned to New Zealand as the regional representatives of W.B.T. in Auckland.

Once the youngest in the family had established his independence, they accepted a new assignment in the Central African Republic, first proceeding to Europe to learn French.

In 1991, Graham and Margaret began their work in the Central African Republic. They learned to cope with the intense heat and humidity, with isolation from their children and grandchildren, and with susceptibility to malaria and other tropical diseases. The country's shaky economy and its reliance on military force to maintain control produced a hostile environment in which to live and work. They were also victims of an armed robbery which left them beaten, bruised, and bereft of their possessions.

1996 saw several military uprisings, one of which resulted in the evacuation of most expatriates.

During these difficult years, Margaret coped also with Parkinson's disease. In this booklet she tells how her uncertainties and anxieties have been transformed by God's power into a new awareness of His presence and love. Though limited by her symptoms, Margaret is joyful in hope, knowing that in God's perfect time the healing she asked for will become a reality. *He knows whether it will be here or in heaven.*

Graham and Margaret James

Chapter One

DISCOVERING

GOD'S

PLAN

Discovering God's Plan

My life began in New Zealand, one of the most beautiful countries in the world. I grew up on a dairy farm and from my birth enjoyed good health. I seldom visited the family doctor, and for as long as I can remember I tried to avoid taking medicine. I preferred letting my body fight any illnesses that came my way.

In 1988, shortly after celebrating my fiftieth birthday, this philosophy of mine seemed to stop working. For no apparent reason my shoulder kept bothering me, and I began to wonder if it was a sign of old age. So I asked a friend in the medical profession what she thought this ache in my shoulder might be. In her opinion, it was "painful arc" syndrome, and in a matter of time the pain should subside. After tolerating the discomfort for almost a year, I was delighted and relieved when her prognosis proved correct. Little did I know that this seemingly trivial symptom was an early indication of more serious problems to come.

In 1990, another symptom developed that was even more bothersome than my sore shoulder had been. Without any provocation, my hands started shaking. At the time, my husband Graham and I were in Switzerland learning French, preparing for an assignment in the Central African Republic. We assumed this shaking was related to stress, since language studies had put pressure on me. So we decided I should withdraw from formal lessons and continue learning the language on an informal basis. Living in Neuchâtel where the Swiss speak French gave me a good grasp of the language before we moved on to Africa.

After we arrived in the Central African Republic this tremor continued, and my next observation was that my handwriting was becoming smaller. Unknown to me, my walking pattern had also changed and I frequently stumbled over one foot as I walked. While walking one day with our African friends, it suddenly dawned on me that I was not swinging my arms. Thinking this may have been a contributing factor, I made a conscious effort

3

to swing them from that day onward. Although this helped me regain some vitality, it did not resolve my walking problem.

In April 1992, when we were engaged in a village project, we were joined in the guest house by a doctor from another mission. He had been flown in by plane to perform major surgery at the local hospital. While eating breakfast one morning, we asked if we could discuss my problem with him. He began by asking us if we were aware of my illness. Taken aback by our ignorance, he said he had diagnosed it the first day. It was obvious to him that I was suffering from Parkinson's disease.

Wow! The diagnosis was given as simply as that! Before going to surgery, the doctor loaned us his medical book, inviting us to read the section on Parkinson's. As we read it together, I was overcome with shock, for I was able to identify with all the listed symptoms. My heart missed a beat when we discovered further on that this particular disease has no known cure.

When its full significance finally sank in, I was totally numbed. For several days I was plagued with questions. Would Parkinson's disease cause my life to be shortened? Was it going to make me dependent on others? How would it affect my relationship with Graham? Could we continue our work in Central Africa? Must I take medicine for the rest of my life? (I shuddered at the thought!) Would I become a burden to my family?

With questions like these filling my mind, I felt like a victim of circumstance. Being God's child, I knew this was false. Nothing touches my life by chance. Every circumstance I encounter is part of God's will — a truth I had learned 25 years before.

When Sonja, our eldest child, was three and a half years old, she fell from a fire escape and fractured her skull. For the following five days she lay in a coma in the Intensive Care Unit at the Wellington Hospital. Only a month previously our third child, Katie, had been born. The month prior to that, my father had died, just a week after he had been diagnosed with leukemia. Sitting beside Sonja in her unconscious state, I cried out to Jesus asking for help. He answered my prayer as I was reading Matthew chapter 10. The assurance Jesus gave His disciples filled *me* with assurance as well.

"Are not two sparrows sold for a penny? Yet not one of them will fall to the ground apart from the will of your Father." Matthew 10:29

This verse did not say that God made Sonja fall; rather, that her fall was not apart from His will. With my earthly father now in the presence of my heavenly Father, this promise from His Word brought me a double measure of comfort.

Nothing touches my life
by chance.
Every circumstance
I encounter is
part of God's will.

Later that day, my deep anguish was replaced by joy as Sonja regained consciousness and recognized me. When I saw her glance at my pen, I asked her its color. How relieved I was to hear her say it was blue! I praised my Lord for restoring her life and thanked Him, too, that her mind was alert. Due to Sonja's remarkable recovery, she was discharged from the hospital three days later.

In Africa now, as I contemplated my diagnosis, I opened my Bible and reread Matthew chapter 10. Again I was encouraged by what Jesus said. He blessed me anew as I read these two verses:

"And even the very hairs of your head are all numbered. So don't be afraid; you are worth more than many sparrows." Matthew 10:30–31

Reflecting on God's provisions in the past, I knew I could trust Him to provide for the future. Not only was my sickness part of His will, I was also worth more than many sparrows to Him.

Before leaving the village, we asked the doctor for his advice: should we return to New Zealand to seek medical help, or could we remain in the Central African Republic until our furlough at Christmas? In his opinion, staying another nine months would do me no harm, but not being familiar with the details of my case, he preferred not to give us firm advice.

Being sure that God would grant us His wisdom, we asked Him in prayer to guide our decision. More often than not, God directs me through His Word, and on this occasion He did so again.

For the word of God is living and active. Sharper than any double-edged sword, it penetrates even to dividing soul and spirit . . . it judges the thoughts and attitudes of the heart. Hebrews 4:12

Your word is a lamp to my feet and a light to my path. Psalm 119:105

When I read the Bible, God reveals Himself to me and shows me how to enjoy walking with Him. Through the gift of His Son He cleanses me from sin, and through the gift of His Spirit He teaches me His way.

Opening my Bible, I had mixed emotions of being eager, yet anxious, to know what God would say. At the time we were reading through the Gospel of John and were about to begin the eleventh chapter. On reading verse 4, my spirit leaped within me as God's Spirit witnessed to my spirit that this was His message.

When Jesus heard that Lazarus was sick, he said, "This sickness will not end in death. No, it is for God's glory so that God's Son may be glorified through it." John 11:4

As I meditated on these words, I found it hard to imagine how God could be glorified through my having Parkinson's disease. Yet this is precisely what Jesus said about Lazarus: the purpose of his sickness was to bring glory to God's Son. My faith was really challenged by the question posed to Martha when she expressed her indignation at her brother's tomb being opened.

Jesus said, "Did I not tell you that if you believed, you would see the glory of God?" John 11:40

Was I able to believe that God's glory would be seen, even if I have Parkinson's disease until the day I die? My faith in God does not mean He will heal me, because Jesus treats each individual life differently. He knows in what condition I will best glorify Him, whether in sickness or health.

Reflecting on God's
provisions in the past,
I knew I could trust Him
to provide for the future.

While reading chapter 17, I was deeply moved by Jesus' prayer to His Father. Not only did He pray for those who followed Him then, He also prayed for those following Him now. This means that Jesus was praying for me!

"My prayer is not for them alone. I pray also for those who will believe in me through their message." John 17:20

"My prayer is not that you take them out of the world but that you protect them from the evil one." John 17:15

We did not need to pack our bags and fly home, for the prayer Jesus prayed covered our situation. He did not pray that we be taken out of Africa, but rather that His Father would protect us from the evil one. Through this verse the Spirit told me it was okay to stay because the Father would keep me safe in His care.

After we finished reading chapter 21, Graham said with a smile that he thought verse 18 must have been included in John's record especially for me!

"I tell you the truth, when you were younger you dressed yourself and went where you wanted; but when you are old you will stretch out your hands, and someone else will dress you and lead you where

you do not want to go." John 21:18

Although I had not seen any connection between what lay before Peter and what lay before me, this remark by Graham certainly
grabbed my attention. As I read the whole
passage through a second time, it was the final
two words that Jesus addressed to Peter which
stood out to me.

*Jesus said this to indicate the kind of death by which
Peter would glorify God. Then he said to him,
"Follow me!"* John 21:19

When Peter saw the disciple whom Jesus loved
following behind, he immediately asked Jesus
what would happen to him. Like Peter, I had
been thinking about others as well, wondering
how my sickness was going to affect them.
Hence the reply Jesus gave Peter applied to
me too: *I* must focus *my* attention on following Jesus.

*"If I want him to remain alive until I return, what
is that to you? You must follow me."* John 21:22

Jesus insisted that Peter follow, even though He knew of the trauma ahead. By now, Peter knew that he could trust Jesus, whatever might happen.

The first thing I did after hearing the diagnosis was to pray and ask God for healing. I recalled what the angel had said to Mary, when telling her that Elizabeth, her elderly cousin, was pregnant: *"Nothing is impossible with God."* Luke 1:37

When the symptoms continued, I felt abandoned by God. I had expected Him to give me a positive response. Still more questions came flooding to mind: Had God heard the prayer that I offered? Did He work miracles for some people and not others? Did He consider my faith too small, or even more likely, my sins too great? Did I need to persist longer in prayer? Was fasting necessary in order to be healed?

With such questions as these turning over in my mind, God's Spirit within posed this question to me: "If you truly trust Me with all your heart, why can't you trust Me with all your questions?" Gradually I learned to put my questions aside and accept the response that He had given. The Spirit reminded me that when Paul suffered in prison, God used the circumstances to accomplish His plan.

Paul wrote, *"What has happened to me has really served to advance the gospel. Because of my chains, most of the brothers in the Lord have been encouraged to speak the word of God more courageously and fearlessly."* Philippians 1:12, 14

I must focus my attention
on following Jesus.

In his book titled *Fear No Evil*, David Watson, a British evangelist and preacher, recounts his personal struggle with cancer. He writes:

If we have any conception of the greatness of God, we should refrain from pressing the question *Why?* however understandable that might be. On many thousands of issues we simply do not and cannot know. Why does God allow the birth of severely handicapped children? I don't know. Why are some individuals plagued with tragedies for much of their lives, whilst others suffer hardly at all? I don't know. Why is there seeming injustice on every side? I don't know. The questions are endless if we ask *Why?* Instead we should ask the question *What?* "What are you saying to me, God? What are you doing in my life? What response do you want me to make?" With that question we can expect an answer.

It is my conviction that God is always trying to speak to us in his love, even when his word is hard to accept. "Man shall not live by bread alone," said Jesus, "but by every word that proceeds from the mouth of God." This was a quotation from the Old Testament that Jesus used when being tempted by his adversary in the wilderness. More important than anything is knowing God's will and doing it. It is far more important than having intellectual answers to all our philosophical questions about God and man, suffering and pain.

On our return to New Zealand in December 1992, a neurologist confirmed that I had Parkinson's disease. He prescribed a medication that would help control the symptoms, as well as relieve the tension in my muscles. My body would convert this medicine to dopamine, the substance my body lacks. Starting this treatment was a traumatic experience, as every dose taken provoked a battle within me. It wasn't just my reluctance to take drugs or my hatred of the side effects. The inner conflict erupted because I believed God is mighty and could heal me from Parkinson's without the use of medicine.

My doctor, who is a Christian, gently explained that medicine and doctors are tools in God's hand. Not only is God the source of all knowledge, He also created the components of medicine. Thus, instead of being reluctant to take it, I should be thanking God for it and enjoying its benefit.

After having received a warm welcome from our church in Auckland, I asked the church elders if they would pray for my healing. Although we had personally been asking for healing, I wanted to be obedient to the instructions God gave.

Is any one of you sick? He should call the elders of the church to pray over him and anoint him with oil in the name of the Lord. James 5:14

The elders agreed, and a meeting was arranged for the following Sunday at 7:00 am. Waking early, I drew back the curtains and there, spanning the sky, was a magnificent rainbow. This signified to me that God was going to act, and

17

though He did not heal my body at that time, I know He touched my spirit. Indeed, the warmth of His touch that I felt that day is as real to me now as it was the morning they prayed. Not being healed after asking for healing was no longer a problem, for I had come to understand that all of God's responses are a part of His plan.

"For I know the plans I have for you," declares the Lord, "plans to prosper you and not to harm you, plans to give you a hope and a future." Jer. 29:11

Accepting my illness as part of God's plan took a greater step of faith than believing He could heal me. But when I reflected on Jesus' prayer in the Garden, I realized the Father's plan included tremendous suffering for His Son. And despite Jesus knowing His Father could save Him, He chose to accept what His Father had planned.

"Abba, Father, everything is possible for you. Take this cup from me. Yet not what I will, but what you will." Mark 14:36

Since I am committed to following Jesus, I am also committed to accepting His plan.

Being healed from Parkinson's disease is not my first consideration, although humanly speaking I would love to be healed. My highest priority is to please Jesus, my Lord, by trusting Him fully and obeying His commands.

Therefore, since Christ suffered in his body, arm yourselves also with the same attitude, because he who has suffered in his body is done with sin. As a result, he does not live the rest of his earthly life for evil human desires, but rather for the will of God. 1 Peter 4:1–2

Since I am committed to following Jesus, I am also committed to accepting His plan.

My highest priority
is to please
Jesus,
my Lord,
by trusting
Him fully and
obeying His commands.

Chapter Two

DISCOVERING

GOD'S

PURPOSE

Discovering God's Purpose

Provided I am willing, my illness can be God's perfect opportunity to fulfill His purposes in me.

Many passages in Scripture give insight into the specific purpose that God had in mind for certain individuals.

Confront Pharaoh and say to him, "This is what the Lord, the God of the Hebrews, says, 'I have raised you up for this very purpose, that I might show you my power and that my name might be proclaimed in all the earth.'" Exodus 9:13–16

"Men of Israel, listen to this: Jesus . . . was a man accredited by God to you by miracles, wonders and signs, which God did among you through him, as you yourselves know. This man was handed over to you by God's set purpose and foreknowledge; and you, with the help of wicked men, put him to death by nailing him to the cross. But God raised him from the dead. . . ." Acts 2:22–24

22

"For when David had served God's purpose in his own generation, he fell asleep; he was buried with his fathers and his body decayed. But the One whom God raised from the dead did not see decay." Acts 13:36

Though I knew my illness was part of God's plan, I did not know how His purposes would be fulfilled through my illness. As I search for answers, I am discovering God's truth, and knowing the truth means I am being set free — free from anxiety, disappointment, self-pity and despair.

Provided I am willing,
my illness can be
God's perfect opportunity
to fulfill His purpose
in me.

My illness can prompt me to come to God

God's love knows no bounds. Throughout history countless individuals have met the living God because of an illness. For example: Naaman the leper (2 Kings 5); blind Bartimaeus (Mark 10:46); the man with the shriveled hand (Mark 3:1–5); the woman who touched Jesus' cloak (Mark 5:25–34); the paralytic (Mark 2:1–12); and many others.

My illness can test the depth of my faith

When traveling by air, our bags are weighed on the scales at the check-in counter to ensure they comply with the baggage allowance. Similarly, God's servants are weighed on figurative scales to ensure their faith in Him is genuine. When Satan challenged God regarding the true basis of Job's faith, God allowed Satan to strip Job of everything: his possessions, his livestock, his children, and his health. Yet Job's heart was steadfast despite this rigorous testing, proving beyond a doubt that his faith in God was unconditional. See 1 Peter 1:6–7.

My illness can help build my character

Having been made in God's image, I have the freedom to choose. It is for me to decide how I respond to my illness. I can rebel against God in anger or I can cooperate with Him in love. If I choose to do the latter, God will work through it for my good.

We know that in all things God works for the good of those who love him, who have been called according to his purpose. Romans 8:28

Of course, Satan wants me to make a negative response, so that his depraved nature will be seen in me: anger, jealousy, bitterness, immorality, idolatry, lying, selfish ambition, hatred, discord, and the like (Galatians 5:19–21).

However, Jesus wants me to respond positively, so that His Spirit can transform me to reflect His divine nature: love, joy, peace, patience, kindness, goodness, faithfulness, gentleness and self-control (Galatians 5:22).

If my illness is indeed necessary for me to become more like Jesus, I would not exchange my illness for health, wealth or fame. Read 1 Peter 5:10 and James 1:2–4.

We rejoice in our sufferings, because we know that suffering produces perseverance; perseverance, character; and character, hope. And hope does not disappoint us, because God has poured out his love into our hearts by the Holy Spirit, whom he has given us. Romans 5:3–5

My illness can help me to trust in God

Above all else, God wants me to trust Him, no matter what my circumstances may be. In every generation He has delivered His people, telling them not to be afraid but to trust wholly in Him. The command not to be fearful appears in most books of the Bible and was a command that Jesus gave repeatedly. Before going to the cross, He comforted His disciples, saying:

"Do not let your hearts be troubled. Trust in God; trust also in me." John 14:1

Though firm in his faith, Paul claimed that his most severe trial was expressly for the purpose of testing his reliance on God.

Indeed, in our hearts we felt the sentence of death. But this happened that we might not rely on ourselves but on God, who raises the dead. He has delivered us from such a deadly peril, and he will deliver us. 2 Corinthians 1: 9–10

My illness can equip me to give God's comfort to others

Since God is the Comforter, the more like Him I become, the more of His comfort I can give. The comfort God gives me is meant not only for me. It is meant to be given to others facing similar difficulties. I can receive God's comfort through: Jesus, His Son (Hebrews 4:15); the Spirit of truth (John 14:16); the Holy Scriptures (Romans 15:4); and God's servants who themselves have been comforted by Him (2 Corinthians 1:4).

Praise be to the God and Father of our Lord Jesus Christ, the Father of compassion and the God of

all comfort, who comforts us in all our troubles, so that we can comfort those in any trouble with the comfort we ourselves have received from God. For just as the sufferings of Christ flow over into our lives, so also through Christ our comfort overflows.
2 Corinthians 1:3–5

My illness can display the glory of God

On hearing the news that Lazarus was sick, Jesus said his sickness was to glorify God's Son. Six days later, Jesus went to Lazarus' tomb and raised Lazarus up so that people might believe.

Then Jesus looked up and said, "Father, I thank you that you have heard me. I knew that you always hear me, but I said this for the benefit of the people standing here, that they may believe that you sent me." John 11:41–42

When Peter and John healed the man crippled from birth, the people who saw it were simply amazed. The man who used to sit begging at the temple gate called Beautiful was in the temple courts with them, walking and jumping, and praising the Lord. When the people gave the credit to Peter and John, they in turn gave the glory to God.

Peter said to them, "Men of Israel, why does this surprise you? Why do you stare at us as if by our own power or godliness we had made this man walk? The God of Abraham, Isaac and Jacob, the God of our fathers, has glorified his servant Jesus. . . . By faith in the name of Jesus, this man whom you see and know was made strong. It is Jesus' name and the faith that comes through him that has given this complete healing to him, as you can all see." Acts 3:12–16

Another healing that glorified God was that of the man who had been blind from his birth. When the disciples asked their Master whose sin had caused his blindness, Jesus told them plainly that sin was not the problem:

"Neither this man nor his parents sinned, but this happened so that the work of God might be displayed in his life." John 9:3

Jesus' response leaves no room for any doubt. This man's blindness was not due to personal sin. Although sickness originated as a result of the Fall, not every person's sickness is related to sin. The answer Jesus gave serves as a reminder to all: one must not jump to conclusions when someone falls sick! Too often sick people are wrongly accused. Consider what God said concerning Job's three friends (Job 42:7).

When other Christians judge me on account of my illness, I fix my mind on truths such as these: God did not send His Son to condemn the world, but rather to save it (John 3:17); Jesus does not lay charges against those whom God has chosen (Romans 8:33), rather, He is interceding for them at God's right hand (Hebrews 7:25); Satan is the one who accuses them before God day and night (Revelation 12:10); Jesus warns His followers not to judge each other, or they too will be judged (Matthew 7:1).

My illness can be a corrective measure

When Miriam and Aaron criticized Moses for marrying a Cushite and were jealous of him because God spoke only through him, God's anger was such that He afflicted Miriam with leprosy. Seeing the evidence of God's discipline on her, Aaron asked Moses for forgiveness. Moses in turn asked God to heal Miriam.

When the cloud lifted . . . there stood Miriam — leprous, like snow. Aaron said to Moses, "Please, my lord, do not hold against us the sin we have so foolishly committed." So Moses cried out to the Lord, "O God, please heal her!" The Lord replied, "Confine her outside the camp for seven days; after that she can be brought back." Numbers 12:10–14

In the church at Corinth, many were sick and a number had died due to the fact they had not honored the Lord's body. They had participated in the Lord's Supper without recognizing their sin.

Anyone who eats and drinks without recognizing the body of the Lord eats and drinks judgment on himself. That is why many among you are weak and sick, and a number of you have fallen asleep. But if we judged ourselves we would not come under judgment. When we are judged by the Lord, we are being disciplined so that we will not be condemned with the world. 1 Corinthians 11:29–32

My illness can be a learning experience

In God's school of learning, suffering is the course I find the most difficult. Although I commenced in tears, I am continuing in joy. The Holy Spirit is my teacher and encourages me on. The lessons He teaches me are renewing my mind.

In Psalm 119, David testifies of the blessings he received from the afflictions he suffered. He could say from experience, "It was good for me to be afflicted so that I might learn your decrees" (v. 71). Yes, David agrees that pain is gain.

My illness can make me available to become God's special agent

Without God, my illness would not be serving any good purpose. With Him, however, it is changed into a channel of blessing. God is working through my illness to accomplish His purposes, one of which, I believe, is to bring encouragement to others.

When Paul was writing to the churches in Galatia, he declared that an illness had prompted his first visit. While there, he shared the gospel of Christ.

As you know, it was because of an illness that I first preached the gospel to you. Even though my illness was a trial to you, you did not treat me with contempt and scorn. Galatians 4:13–14

A sick Egyptian slave became God's special agent to lead King David and his men to their wives and children in captivity (1 Samuel 30).

When Samaria was under siege, God chose four starving lepers to be His special agents (2 Kings 7). Since the lepers believed that death was inevitable, they were willing to risk entering enemy territory. Discovering the camp deserted, they looked inside the tents and found ample food for all in Samaria. (When becoming God's agent puts my life at risk, the devil very cunningly suggests an alternative.)

Satan used this tactic when he tempted Jesus in the desert, even misquoting Scripture in support of his plans. But Jesus stood firm and refused his proposals, rightly quoting the Scriptures, saying, "It is written . . ." (Matthew 4).

When God's purpose for His Son involved death by crucifixion, Jesus was obedient to His Father's plan. He made no attempt to evade the pain but endured the cross for the sake of man.

When they hurled their insults at him, he did not retaliate; when he suffered, he made no threats. Instead, he entrusted himself to him who judges justly. 1 Peter 2:23

When God's plan for me involves danger or pain, I pray that I will obey for the sake of my Lord.

Chapter Three

DISCOVERING

GOD'S

PERSPECTIVE

Discovering God's Perspective

"For my thoughts are not your thoughts, neither are your ways my ways." Isaiah 55:8

In the light of the above declaration, it stands to reason that God's perspective is not mine either.

From my perspective, having Parkinson's disease is a disappointment and cause for concern. As the disease progresses, my movements slow down. With the slowing down of my movements, my performance declines. Having a lower standard of performance, my frustrations increase. As a result, I feel trapped in a downward spiral.

Satan tries to twist my perspective even further, for *"he is a liar and the father of lies"* (John 8:44). His viewpoint may seem quite reasonable at first, for habitually he starts with an element of truth. Perhaps he will refer to a passage of Scripture, such as Matthew 7:7–8, *"Ask and it will be given you . . . For everyone who asks receives."* His argument may develop like this: Does God really say He will give what you ask? Have you asked Him to heal you from Parkinson's? If you have asked Him, why aren't you healed? If God has not healed you, He has broken His promise. If God doesn't keep His promise, you cannot trust His Word.

By distorting the truth and discrediting Scripture, Satan tries to turn me away from the Lord. Ever since Adam and Eve were created, Satan has made it his goal to separate man from his Maker.

I am thankful to God that Satan's power has been broken by the death and resurrection of Jesus, His Son. Now it is possible for whoever believes in Him to overcome Satan by what He has accomplished.

Jesus shared in their humanity so that by his death he might destroy him who holds the power of death — that is, the devil — and free those who all their

lives were held in slavery by their fear of death.
Hebrews 2:14–15

They overcame him by the blood of the Lamb and by the word of their testimony; they did not love their lives so much as to shrink from death. Revelation 12:11

In reading the Bible, I gain a glimpse of God's viewpoint and see myself as God sees me. If I pay no attention, I am just like a person who looks in a mirror, then forgets what he saw (James 1:23–24). But whether or not I take any notice, God declares this concerning His Word:

"My word will not return to me empty, but will accomplish what I desire and achieve the purpose for which I sent it." Isaiah 55:11

Satan's arguments were completely unfounded. He cannot invalidate the Word of the Lord. The question is not whether God keeps His promise but whether my petition is part of His plan.

Viewing my illness from God's perspective helps build my confidence and dispel my fears. Even though in the physical sense I am progressively becoming weaker, in the spiritual sense I am growing stronger each day. Now I can better understand this message Paul wrote:

Therefore we do not lose heart. Though outwardly we are wasting away, yet inwardly we are being renewed day by day. For our light and momentary troubles are achieving for us an eternal glory that far outweighs them all. So we fix our eyes not on what is seen, but on what is unseen. For what is seen is temporary, but what is unseen is eternal. 2 Corinthians 4:16–18

I cannot see God's perspective by my own natural instinct. Rather, God reveals it to me by means of His Spirit. Jesus told His disciples, after Judas left the Upper Room, that He shows himself only to those who love and obey Him.

"Whoever has my commands and obeys them, he is the one who loves me. He who loves me will be loved by my Father, and I too will love him and show myself to him." John 14:21

> Viewing my illness from
> God's perspective
> helps build my
> confidence
> and dispel my fears.

The contrast between God's perspective and man's is plain in this event recorded in Numbers 13–14:

When the twelve spies returned from Canaan they displayed two opposing perspectives.

The ten said, *"The land we explored devours those living in it. All the people we saw there are of great size. . . . We seemed like grasshoppers in our own eyes, and we looked the same to them."* Numbers 13:32–33

Whereas Joshua and Caleb said, *"The land we passed through and explored is exceedingly good. If the Lord is pleased with us, he will lead us into that land. . . . Do not be afraid of the people . . . the Lord is with us."* Numbers 14:7–9

Joshua and Caleb viewed the situation from God's perspective, while the other ten saw it from their own point of view. Sadly, their view prevailed and the whole Israelite community spent the next forty years wandering in the desert. By refusing to trust God, all that generation, except for Joshua and Caleb, forfeited their right to enter the promised land. A journey started in victory ended in defeat!

As I reflect on this dramatic event, it is easy for me to point a finger at the Israelites and criticize them for their vote of no confidence in God. But how do I measure up in my world today? From whose perspective do I look at my illness? Surely I have more reason to trust God fully than did the Israelites who lived long ago. When I think of the miracles He performed to deliver me from my sin, they are every bit as remarkable as the measures He took to deliver them from their slavery.

Think of it: God became flesh and was born of a virgin. He was given the name Jesus and grew in stature and in wisdom. He was tempted by Satan, yet He committed no sin. He died on a cross and was buried in a tomb. The third day He arose and appeared to His disciples. Since God can accomplish all these miracles and more, surely I can trust Him with the sickness I have.

Not only this, but unlike the Israelites, God has given me His Spirit to be my Helper and Guide.

"And I will ask the Father, and he will give you another Counselor to be with you forever — the Spirit of truth. The world cannot accept him, because it neither sees him nor knows him. But you know him, for he lives with you and will be in you." John 14:16–17

I can face any challenge with God's Spirit within, for He gives me strength in weakness, victory in temptation, courage in difficulty, peace in turmoil, joy in grief, love in conflict, comfort in sorrow, hope in despair, and life in death.

The question is not
whether God keeps
His promise,
but whether
my petition is
part of His plan.

I can face any challenge
with God's Spirit within,
for He gives me
strength in weakness,
victory in temptation,
courage in difficulty,
peace in turmoil,
joy in grief,
love in conflict,
comfort in sorrow,
hope in despair,
and life in death.

Chapter Four

DISCOVERING

GOD'S

PASSION

Discovering God's Passion

A new day dawned, August 22, 1964 — the day we exchanged our wedding vows. We both vowed to love and cherish each other: for better, for worse; for richer, for poorer; in sickness and in health. When we uttered these vows, I would never have imagined that from the age of fifty I would be in sickness rather than health. (I would probably have put myself in one of the previous two categories!)

Although my illness is robbing me of my health, it is certainly not robbing me of the love of my husband. But even if Graham's love for me were influenced by it, God's love for me can never be taken away. His love is unconditional, unlimited, and eternal.

Who shall separate us from the love of Christ? Shall trouble or hardship or persecution or famine or nakedness or danger or sword? As it is written: "For your sake we face death all day long; we are

46

*considered as sheep to be slaughtered." No, in all
these things we are more than conquerors through
him who loved us. For I am convinced that neither
death nor life, neither angels nor demons, neither
the present nor the future, nor any powers, neither
height nor depth, nor anything else in all creation,
will be able to separate us from the love of God
that is in Christ Jesus.* Romans 8:35–39

Christians can unknowingly put God's love into
question. Since having this illness, I have heard
comments like these: a God who loves you
could not let you suffer; sickness is not the
will of God; your healing will come as a sign
of His blessing; you will be healed from your
sickness if you appropriate Christ's death, for
it says in His Word we are healed by His
wounds.

Initially such comments were very disturbing,
for they threatened the very core of my faith.
But the Scriptures tell me what I must do: I
am to give all my worries to Jesus and leave
them there.

Humble yourselves, therefore, under God's mighty hand, that he may lift you up in due time. Cast all your anxiety on him because he cares for you. 1 Peter 5:6–7

Jesus showed me the extent of His care when He died on the cross to pay the debt for my sins. I do not need healing to be sure of God's love; Jesus' death proved His love for me, once and for all.

This is how we know what love is: Jesus Christ laid down his life for us. And we ought to lay down our lives for our brothers. 1 John 3:16

For God so loved the world that he gave his one and only Son, that whoever believes in him shall not perish but have eternal life. John 3:16

In writing to the churches both in Galatia and in Corinth, Paul made reference to an illness he had. When he asked for healing, he was given grace — the grace he needed to continue his ministry.

As you know, it was because of an illness that I first preached the gospel to you. Even though my illness was a trial to you, you did not treat me with contempt or scorn. Galatians 4:13–14

To keep me from becoming conceited because of these surpassingly great revelations, there was given me a thorn in my flesh, a messenger of Satan, to torment me. Three times I pleaded with the Lord to take it away from me. But he said, "My grace is sufficient for you, for my power is made perfect in weakness." 2 Corinthians 12:7–9

I do not need healing
to be sure of God's love;
Jesus' death proved
His love for me,
once and for all.

Even though Paul was not given physical healing, he became God's agent to bring healing to others.

Publius' father was sick in bed, suffering from fever and dysentery. Paul went in to see him and, after prayer, placed his hands on him and healed him. When this had happened, the rest of the sick on the island came and were cured. Acts 28:7–9

On the first day of the week we came together to break bread. Paul spoke to the people and, because he intended to leave the next day, kept on talking until midnight. . . . Seated in a window was a young man named Eutychus, who was sinking into a deep sleep as Paul talked on and on. When he was sound asleep, he fell to the ground from the third story and was picked up dead. Paul went down, threw himself on the young man and put his arms around him. "Don't be alarmed," he said. "He's alive!" Then Paul went upstairs again and broke bread and ate. After talking until daylight, he left. The people took the young man home alive and were greatly comforted. Acts 20:7–12

Not everyone in Paul's company was necessarily healed. Trophimus, his companion, had to be put ashore at Miletus, due to the fact he was too sick to sail on.

Erastus stayed in Corinth, and I left Trophimus sick in Miletus. 2 Timothy 4:20

When Paul wrote to the Philippians, he reported that Epaphroditus, whom they had sent to help him, had been seriously ill. However, God in His mercy had spared him from dying. Though Paul did not elaborate on his present state of health, he said he felt it necessary to send Epaphroditus back home. In taking this action, Paul said he himself would be less anxious, and the Philippians, on seeing Epaphroditus again, would be very glad.

But I think it is necessary to send back to you Epaphroditus, my brother, fellow worker . . . whom you sent to take care of my needs. For he longs for all of you and is distressed because you heard he was ill. Indeed he was ill, and almost died. But God had mercy on him, and not on him only but also on me, to spare me sorrow upon sorrow. There-fore I am all the more eager to send him, so that when you see him again you may be glad and I may have less anxiety. Philippians 2:25–28

The Philippians loved Epaphroditus very deeply, and his illness in no way diminished their love. In actuality, the opposite was true. Hearing of his illness, they longed to see him all the more.

If mere human love can be so strong, how could I imagine God's love to be less? Of course, Satan keeps insisting that if God really loved me, He would heal me from Parkinson's. But when Satan lies, he speaks his native language (John 8:44).

While recently reading *A Gentle Thunder* by Max Lucado, I gained a new appreciation for the value of suffering. He writes:

> How far do you want God to go in getting your attention? If God has to choose between your eternal safety

and your earthly comfort, which do you hope he chooses? Don't answer too quickly. Give it some thought. . . .

God does what it takes to get our attention. Isn't that the message of the Bible? . . . The relentless pursuit of God. God on the hunt. God in the search. . . . God is creative as he is relentless. . . . Both kind and stern. Tender and tough. Faithfully firm.

God will whisper. He will shout. He will touch and tug. He will take away our burdens; he'll even take away our blessings. If there are a thousand steps between us and him, he will take all but one. But he will leave the final one for us. The choice is ours.

Please understand. His goal is not to make you happy. His goal is to make you his. His goal is not to get you what you want; it is to get you what you need. And if that means a jolt or two to get you in your seat, then be jolted. Earthly discomfort is a glad swap for heavenly peace.

Being diagnosed with Parkinson's disease was a jolt indeed, but it caused my ear to become more attentive to God's voice. I have heard Him say in a variety of ways that in every situation He is working for my good. God's plan and purpose is not to make me suffer; rather, it is to transform me into the image of His Son.

And we know that in all things God works for the good of those who love him, who have been called according to his purpose. For those God foreknew he also predestined to be conformed to the likeness of his Son. Romans 8:28–29

> ## Earthly discomfort
> ## is a glad swap
> ## for heavenly peace.

> God's plan for me
> is not to make me suffer;
> rather, it is
> to transform me
> into the image
> of His Son.

Walking with Jesus along the road of discovery has lifted my burden and strengthened my faith. Following Him, I place my feet in His footprints, knowing each step I take He has already taken. Thankfully, my future is known only to Him, and my present is filled with His love, peace and joy.

The Lord's compassions never fail. They are new every morning; great is your faithfulness. I say to myself, "The Lord is my portion; therefore I will wait for him." The Lord is good to those whose hope is in him, to the one who seeks him; it is good to wait quietly for the salvation of the Lord. Lamentations 3:22–26

Discovering God's plan, purpose, perspective and passion plucked me out of the "downward spiral." With what better words could I finish my story than with the words of Paul after he was given God's grace: *"Therefore, I will boast all the more gladly about my weaknesses, so that Christ's power may rest on me."* 2 Corinthians 12:9

I asked for healing . . .
                                      but was given grace

May God give you insight as you seek to discover what His **plan, purpose,** and **perspective** are in regard to your illness. Remember always: God's **passion** is profound and His **grace** is guaranteed.

Thankfully,
my future
is known
only to Him,
and my present
is filled
with His love,
peace,
and joy.

"My grace is
sufficient for you,
for my power
is made perfect
in weakness."

2 Corinthians 12:9

Acknowledgements

Page v

Quotation from *On Pain: Beyond Suffering* by Kenneth L. Pike, © Summer Institute of Linguistics, Dallas, TX, used by permission.

Pages 15–16

Quotation from *Fear No Evil* by David Watson, © Harold Shaw Publishers, Wheaton, IL, used by permission.

Pages 52–54

Quotation from *A Gentle Thunder* by Max Lucado, © Word Inc., Dallas, TX. All rights reserved. Used by permission.

This book was produced by the Christian Literature Crusade. We hope it has been helpful to you in living the Christian life. CLC is a literature mission with ministry in over 50 countries worldwide. If you would like to know more about us, or are interested in opportunities to serve with a faith mission, we invite you to write to:

Christian Literature Crusade
P.O. Box 1449
Fort Washington, PA 19034